With Love

To

From

Daughter

new seasons™

Original inspirations by Susan Letham, Jennifer John Ouellette, Donna Shryer, and Lynda Twardowski. Other quotes compiled by Joan Loshek.

Picture credits:
Front cover (inset) illustrated by Denise Hilton Campbell.
Book jacket illustrated by Robin Moro.
© **Artbeats Digital Film Library**; © **Brand X Pictures**; **Bridgeman Art Library**: Private Collection/Phillips, Fine Art Auctioneers, New York, USA/Bridgeman Art Library; © **Corbis**; **Corbis**: © Blue Lantern Studio, © Philadelphia Museum of Art, © Swim Ink; © **Getty Images**; © **Planet Art**; © **Stockbyte**; **SuperStock**: © Christian Pierre

Acknowledgments:
Publications International, Ltd., has made every effort to locate the owners of all copyrighted material to obtain permission to use the selections that appear in this book. Any errors or omissions are unintentional; corrections, if necessary, will be made in future editions.

From the book *A Toolbox for Our Daughters*. Copyright © 2000 by Annette Geffert and Diane Brown. Reprinted with permission of New World Library, Novato, California.

Excerpted from *Between Mother & Daughter* by Judy and Amanda Ford with permission of Conari Press, an imprint of Red Wheel/Weiser.

New Seasons is a trademark of Publications International, Ltd.

Louis Weber, CEO
Publications International, Ltd.
7373 N. Cicero Avenue
Lincolnwood, Illinois 60712

www.pilbooks.com

Permission is never granted for commercial purposes.

Manufactured in China.

8 7 6 5 4 3 2 1

ISBN: 1-4127-0311-5

As I've watched you climb trees and skin your knees, you have taught me how strong a woman can be.

I cradled you in my arms for a while, but I'll hold you in my heart forever.

Never fear what the world may bring.
Its gifts will far outweigh its troubles.
How do I know? Because it brought me you.

I knew you were grown up when you stopped
talking about dreams as pictures you saw in
the night and started talking about them as
what you had in mind for your life.

I didn't get to choose you.
I was just plain lucky.

You have worked so hard to be the
perfect daughter. But, in my eyes, you
were born perfect.

our photo

A family blessed with a daughter is a home
filled with laughter.

The two greatest mysteries
life? How one little girl can
be so messy, and when she
grows up, how that messy
little girl can be so missed.

You were the only person with the ability to wake me in the wee hours with an ear-piercing wail and still manage to get me to smile before the sun rose.

The secrets of the universe were thought to be hidden among the stars. Now common theory is they're just with everything else that's hard to find . . . in a daughter's closet.

You have given me so much . . . not the least of which is fashion advice.

How to weather life:
Share your sunny
disposition, your bright
smile, and your breezy
welcome with everyone
you meet.

What's love like? It's like this: Being loved
will make you feel light enough to fly up
and out into the world. Loving someone
will help you find your way home again.

your photo

I adored the child
you were, embraced the
girl you became, and stand in awe of the woman you are.

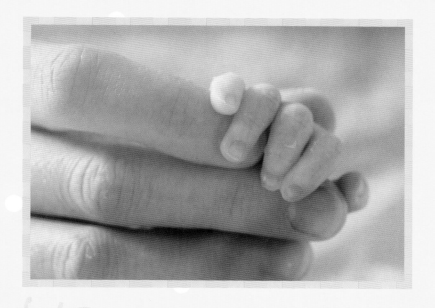

There is no other closeness in human life
like the closeness between a mother and her
baby—chronologically, physically, and
spiritually they are just a few heartbeats
away from being the same person.

SUSAN CHEEVER

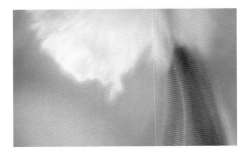

*W*here do mothers learn all the things
they tell their daughters not to do?

EVAN ESAR

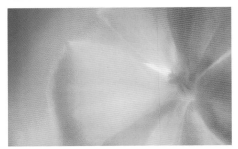

A daughter may borrow her parents' car,
but she'll surely steal their hearts.

The relationship between mothers and children never changes, and that's because no matter how rich or powerful you are, your mother still remembers when you were three and put SpaghettiOs up your nose.

DENNIS MILLER

True satisfaction is knowing that even if
you were wealthy and powerful, you
wouldn't change a thing about your life.

You twirl and dance, completely one with the music. Good living is like that; you need to go with the beat. Sometimes life calls you to dance a breathless polka and sometimes a dignified waltz. Just move in time to the music, and you'll get it right.

When you were small, you taught me how to live in the moment. I'd ask you, "What's your favorite time of year?" and you'd think for a moment and answer, "this one." That's a pretty wonderful way to live life.

A parent is powerless against only two things:
pigtails and the little girl wearing them.

your photo

Before you were born, I pictured how you would look, how
you would act, and who you would become when you grew up.
You are more beautiful than I ever imagined.

A daughter is like a boomerang: Her parents send her to venture off on her own and are exhilarated each time she is back in their arms.

Each child has one extra line to [a parent's] heart, which no other child can replace.

MARGUERITE KELLY AND ELIA PARSONS

The first time I understood the power of unconditional love was when you put on my favorite (and expensive!) pair of shoes.

Love is that condition in which the happiness of another person is essential to your own.

ROBERT A. HEINLEIN

What a grand thing, to be loved! What a grander thing still, to love!

VICTOR HUGO

I knew you were
spreading your wings
when you started
asking about the past.
A woman needs to
understand where
she's coming from so
she can better choose
where she wants to go.

"What will you give the world," they asked me? For years I wondered; today I know: My gift is you.

*L*ove never claims, it ever gives.

MOHANDAS K. GANDHI

I taught you a thing or two, but you should know you taught me, too.

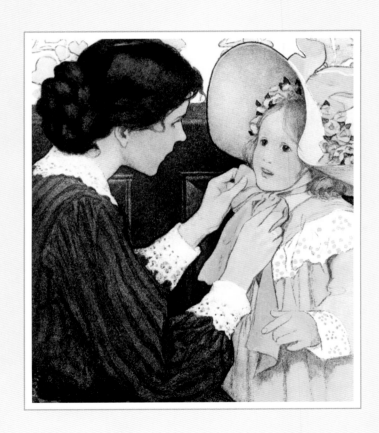

I will always see you as my little girl.

There are few things in life more difficult than raising a daughter. There is nothing more rewarding.

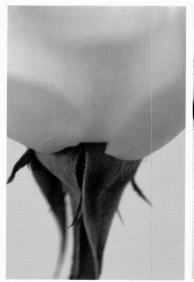

our photo

The love between a parent and daughter
is strong enough to weather the storms
on the sea of life.

The essence of love is kindness.

ROBERT LOUIS STEVENSON

I didn't lose a daughter when you grew up. I gained a friend.

When you were young, you used to wander away sometimes, and I would have trouble finding you for a few moments. But then you would catch my eye, and the world was right. I still never want to lose sight of you.

I may not be rich in worldly ways, but you can always bank on my love and support.

The pride in having a daughter is not like that of owning a car or a home. Once the new car smell subsides or the fresh paint dries, the pride fades, too. With a daughter, years can go by, and then the parents look at her as if it were the first time. They want to stand on a chair and proudly exclaim, "She's mine!"

You give me a million reasons
to glow with pride.

The moment a little girl is born, her parents' emotions become sewn together with her's. If someone hurts her, they ache. If someone teases her, they cry. If someone compliments her, they give thanks. It is this deep connection that is strengthened as they all age.

I live for those who
love me, for those who
know me true.

GEORGE LINNAEUS BANKS

It's funny how things come full circle. When we were young and coping with you as a tired two-year-old, we'd give anything for two minutes alone. But now that you are grown, we treasure the opportunities to have two minutes alone...with you.

I will never forget the day you were born,
for on that day I was born, too.

No matter your profession, your first full-time job was as my daughter and you were—and are—a success!

I love you for who you are, not what you've done.

Change means moving beyond our comfort zones. We sure helped each other do that over the years. Maybe that's why we feel so close now that you're grown.

The butterfly has
flown. I watch you
soar and marvel at
the lovely creature
you've become.

A daughter is her parents' contribution
to a better world.

Give a little love to a
child, and you get a
great deal back.

JOHN RUSKIN

Daughters bring joy to the heart, laughter to the lips, and gray hairs to the head.

The happiest moments of my life have
been the few which I have passed at home
in the bosom of my family.

THOMAS JEFFERSON

Being a parent is the next best thing to being a kid again! With you I relived my own childhood years. You have kept me young and reminded me how to live life to the fullest.

A daughter's fingerprints on furniture, windows, and walls leave traces of love scribbled around the margins of a parent's heart.